COPYRIGHT © 2025 ROCK YOU PUBLISHING, LLC.

All rights reserved. This book contains material protected under International and Federal Copyright Laws and Treaties. Any unauthorized reprint or use of this material is prohibited. No part of this book may be reproduced or transmitted in any form or by any means, electronic or mechanical, including photocopying, recording, or by any information storage and retrieval system without express written permission from the author. The Library of Congress has a record of this publication. This publication was printed in the United States of America.

ISBN: 9798271547782

For information about permission to reproduce selections from this book contact the author:

Adrienne Draper at: www.adriennedraper.com

THIS BOOK IS INSPIRED BY ALL THE FUN I HAD PREPARING FOR HOLIDAYS AS A KID.

-ADRIENNE DRAPER

**Every autumn leaves fall in many different colors,
A sign a holiday is near where I help my grandmother.**

We take a ride to the countryside in boots and overalls,
To pick the most delicious apples and pumpkins we can haul.

Outside we place pumpkins, a doormat and a wreath,
Orange, green and hint of cream pillows on the porch swing.

Inside the smell of pumpkin spice and cinnamon itch my nose.
I freshen up, put my apron on and to the kitchen I go.

Grandpa's in the dining room setting the table for Thanksgiving,

**Trees now shimmer snowflakes, as ice cycles line the gutters.
I lay and sway my arms and legs making snow angels with my mother.**

Grandpa pulls up, in his pick up truck and says, "You're coming with me."
We take a drive to the countryside to pick the perfect tree.

Some are tall, some are wide, they all are pointy and prick.

The most beautiful tree is evergreen, I said, "Grandpa this is it!"

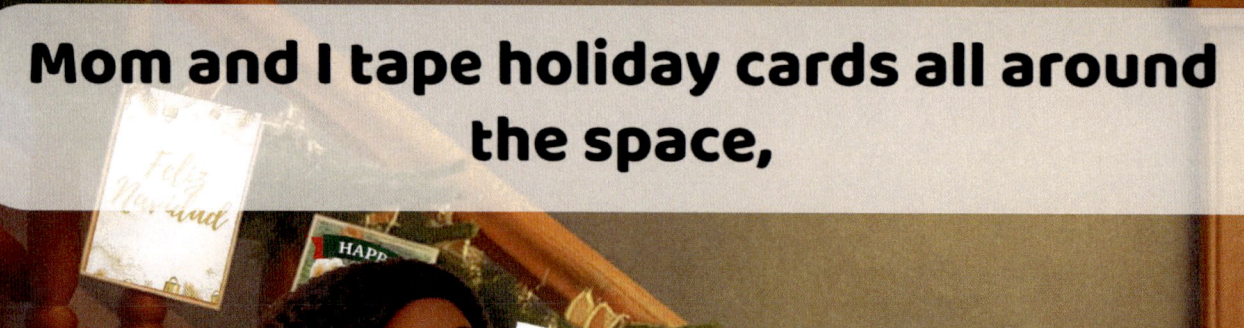

Mom and I tape holiday cards all around the space,

Arranging fruit, nuts, and mints like when she was my age.

Flowers blossom, flowers bloom, sunflowers grow taller than me.

My grandparents and I paint boiled eggs for fun and to distract,

While mom and dad hide plastic eggs in the yard out back.

Holidays are special times to gather with one another,
Especially when the sweetest treat is helping my grandmother.

Seasons

Down
1. leaves fall from trees
2. plants begin to grow

Across
2. hottest time of year
3. cold snowy weather

Winter Holidays

Directions: Draw a line to match the holiday symbol.

Egg Maze

Can you solve the maze?

Start

Finish

HOLIDAY WORD SEARCH

```
F L O W E R S S E I T L
A H V R M I N K P V H E
P O E E U S O G U I A A
A L R A E A W E M R N V
R I A T S I F N P O K E
T A L H V W L M K I S S
M U L S I A A T I M G S
E T S H L C K B N N I P
N U V V L C E I S K V R
T M N T A C S D O T I I
M N B L O S S O M E N N
G A R D E N I N G H G G
```

BLOSSOM   LEAVES   FLOWERS   THANKSGIVINGG
GARDENING   SPRING   PUMPKINS   OVERALLS
AUTUMN   HOLIDAY   WREATH   SNOWFLAKESS

SEASONS GLOSSARY

AUTUMN/FALL: DAYS GET COOLER, LEAVES CHANGE COLORS AND FALL FROM TREES, AND THINGS LIKE PUMPKINS AND ACORNS ARE COMMON.

SPRING: FLOWERS BLOOM, PLANTS GROW NEW LEAVES, AND BABY ANIMALS ARE BORN.

SUMMER: DAYS ARE HOT AND LONG, PERFECT FOR ACTIVITIES LIKE SWIMMING, CAMPING, AND EATING ICE CREAM.

WINTER: DAYS ARE COLD, AND THERE CAN BE SNOW OR RAIN. PEOPLE WEAR WARM CLOTHES LIKE GLOVES AND SCARVES.

TEMPERATURE: HOW HOT OR COLD IT IS

DID YOU KNOW...

"JINGLE BELLS" WAS THE FIRST SONG EVER PLAYED IN SPACE IN 1965.

DID YOU KNOW...

THE WHITE HOUSE HAS HOSTED AN ANNUAL EASTER EGG ROLL SINCE 1878.

DID YOU KNOW...

HALLOWEEN STARTED OVER 2,000 YEARS AGO MARKING THE END OF HARVEST AND THE START OF WINTER.

ABOUT THE AUTHOR

ACCLAIMED AUTHOR, POET, ACADEMIC, AND MENTAL HEALTH MESSENGER WHO LEVERAGES HER SOCIAL AND PROFESSIONAL INFLUENCES TO ENSURE EQUITABLE EDUCATIONAL ADVANTAGES FOR MARGINALIZED YOUTH. SHE RECEIVED HER BACHELOR'S DEGREE IN PUBLIC COMMUNICATIONS FROM MISSOURI BAPTIST UNIVERSITY, HER MASTER OF FINE ARTS IN CREATIVE WRITING FROM LINDENWOOD UNIVERSITY, AND HER TEACHING ARTIST CERTIFICATE FROM THE TEACHING ARTIST INSTITUTE FROM THE REGIONAL ARTS COMMISSION.

Made in the USA
Coppell, TX
21 November 2025